Enchanted English
Ages 5-6
Alison Head

Aurora is a griffin. She can fly high above the Enchanted Forest and often takes Finn for a ride.

Sparkle, Gem, Dusty and *Firefly* are four playful fairies who live in the bluebell fields.

Professor Willow is a wise old gentleman, who loves to gather facts for his Book of Knowledge.

Gribbit and *Periwinkle* are naughty pixies who play tricks on the fairies with some help from their bug friends.

Finn is an elf prince, who is mastering the art of living in harmony with nature before he becomes king.

Pearl is a unicorn who lives by the Lake of Wisdom. She loves to travel and shares her stories with the forest creatures.

PLEASE DO NOT WRITE IN THIS BOOK – Use your own paper to work through the questions. THANK YOU

Welcome to the Enchanted Forest

Contents

D1337684

9030 00001 6270 3

The alphabet

My name is Professor Willow and I am going to tell you about the alphabet. There are 26 letters in our alphabet and we arrange them in a special order. This makes them easier to remember and means that we can write letters in an order that everyone understands. It is as easy as A-B-C!

The letters a, e, i, o and u are called vowels. The rest are called consonants.

1 **Some letters have disappeared from the Book of Knowledge. See if you can write them in again.**

a b c _ e f _ h _ j k l _ n o
p _ r s t _ v _ x y _

2 **These leaves have all fallen from an alphabet tree. Can you write them in alphabetical order on the blank leaves?**

r   a   f   p   b   k

3 Wonderful work! Now take a look at these words. Each word starts with a different letter of the alphabet. Use this first letter to put the words in alphabetical order.

dog   apple   cat   ball

_____   _____   _____   _____

4 Can you remember which letters are vowels? See if you can circle them.

a b c d e f g h i j k l m n
o p q r s t u v w x y z

Willow's Quest

Work your magic on this invisible picture by joining up the letters in alphabetical order. Then colour in the picture with your favourite crayons.

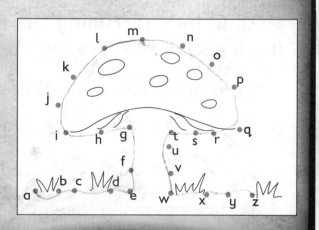

Find the map at the back of the book and add the sticker of my Book of Knowledge.

Plurals

We are Periwinkle and Gribbit.
One pixie is great, but two are better!
Plural means two or more of something.
When you want to write about a plural,
you can often just add s.

tree   trees   owl   owls

1 **Let's get busy! Add s to each of these words to make the plural.**

a bug _s_   b bird _s_   c frog _s_

d lake _s_   e flower _s_

2 **Help us by underlining the right word in the brackets to finish each sentence. Bugalicious!**

a Pearl has three lovely pink sea (shell / shells).

b A (squirrel / squirrels) ran up the tree.

c Sparkle and Dusty collected five pretty (stones / stone).

d Willow has many (pile / piles) of books.

e Finn found a huge (conker / conkers) in the forest.

3 **Now look at each picture and colour in the correct box for what you see.**

a

book	books

b

webs	web

c

rabbits	rabbit

d

moon	moons

e

bat	bats

Willow's Quest

See if you can add these plural things to the pongy picture of the Enchanted Forest. Then colour in your picture with your favourite crayons.

a worms

b snails

c hedgehogs

d mushrooms

e clouds

 Add the sticker of the rabbit and squirrel to the map.

ing verbs

Swish, swish! I am Pearl. Verbs are very useful words that tell us what is happening. If something is happening right now, the verb often ends ing.

Finn (is) walk(ing).

Verbs which describe what is happening now are called present tense verbs.

is are was were

1 Now see if you can complete these word sums. Take your time.

suffix

a see + (ing) =   She is seeing,

b wish + (ing) =   I am wishing

c learn + (ing) =   He is learning

d draw + (ing) =   They are drawing

e buy + (ing) =   We are buying

2 Look carefully at these sentences. Circle the (ing) verbs that describe what is happening now.

a Gribbit is (waiting) for Periwinkle.

b Sparkle and Firefly are (picking) flowers.

c Gribbit is (throwing) stones into the lake.

d Professor Willow is (reading) the Book of Knowledge.

e Aurora is (flying) over the Lake of Wisdom.

3 Choose an **ing** verb from the box to complete each sentence.

| falling looking drinking sleeping being going |

a Gem is ___looking___ into the magic mirror.

b ___drinking___ water from the Lake of Wisdom makes you clever.

hey c Periwinkle and Gribbit say that ___being___ a pixie is fun.

d It is autumn in the Enchanted Forest and leaves are ___falling___ from the trees.

sleep

e The rabbits are ___sleeping___ in their burrows.

den

f Pearl is ___going___ on a long journey.

Willow's Quest

With a swish of your tail, join up these pictures with the correct ing verb.

a singing

b jumping

c crying

d barking

e painting

Add the sticker of the unicorns to the map.

ck endings

We are Gem and Sparkle. The letters c and k are such good friends that you will often see them together at the end of words.

neck   pick   click

Read these words out loud so that you can hear the ck sound. Magic!

1 Now wave your wand and add a **ck** ending to each of these words.

a ba_ck_   d sho_ck_

b si_ck_   e lo_ck_

c fli_ck_   f pa_ck_

2 Write down the **ck** word to match each picture.

a

Sock

b

a box

c

a tick

d

a clock

e

cick

f

sgck

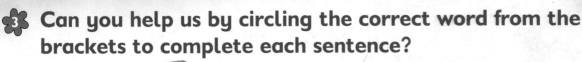

3 Can you help us by circling the correct word from the brackets to complete each sentence?

a A large (**black** / blac) spider ran across the floor.

b Making a wish in the Enchanted Forest brings good (luc / **luck**).

c Professor Willow heard a (knok / **knock**) at his door.

d The fairies (**pick** / pic) flowers in the Magic Meadow.

e Professor Willow has a huge (**stack** / stak) of books.

f A (flok / **flock**) of birds flew over the forest.

g Gribbit showed Pearl a magic (**trick** / tric).

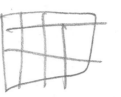

Willow's Quest

See if you can find these **ck** words in the word search. Flit, flit!

block   crack

quick   track

click

q	u	i	c	k
h	c	g	f	k
t	r	a	c	k
c	a	e	l	i
o	c	e	i	d
b	k	w	c	o
c	e	j	k	t
b	l	o	c	k

Pop the bluebells sticker on the map. Flit, flit!

Magic e

When it is at the end of some words, the magical letter e can change the sound made by vowels in the middle of the word. Remember, vowels are a, e, i, o and u.

Read these words out loud.

hop   hope

Can you see how adding the magic e has changed the sound made by the o in the word hope?

1 **Underline the word in each sentence that ends with a magic e.**

a Gem found a pretty stone.

b A rabbit ran down the lane.

c Periwinkle and Gribbit enjoy the same foods.

d Gribbit climbed a pine tree.

e The squirrel gathered a pile of acorns.

2 **Let's get busy! Now complete the word sums to change the vowel sounds in these words.**

a tap + e = _tape_   d rip + e = _ripe_

b hid + e = _hide_   e strip + e = _stripe_

c cap + e = _cape_   f rat + e = _rate_

3 Write sentences containing each of these magic e words.

a hole The fox dug a deep hole.

b line We are writing for our parents on the line.

c alone Little Beaver live all alone but he did not have any brother

d time and sister. Its time to go to tesco.

e made Britbney and sophia made fries for lunch to eat.

Willow's Quest

Now try writing labels for these objects.

a
bone

b
Icecream

c
gate

d
rope

e
plate

Light

Add the sticker of the mice fishing, Bugalicious!

11

ed verbs

Iam Finn and I want to tell you about ed verbs. Verbs tell us what is happening but they can also tell us when something happened. If something has already happened, the verb will often end ed.

look   looked

Verbs that tell us that something has already happened are called past tense verbs.

1 **Try these word sums, word warrior.**

a reach + ed = _reached_

b cook + ed = _cooked_

c wait + ed = _waited_

d listen + ed = _listened_

e paint + ed = _painted_

2 **Underline the past tense ed verb in each sentence.**

a The fairies watched the sun set.

b Gribbit laughed at Periwinkle.

c The frog gobbled up a fly.

d Pearl galloped through the forest.

e Professor Willow turned the page in the Book of Knowledge.

3 Now that you have mastered adding ed, try circling the past tense ed verbs in this group.

washed

try

speak

hop

shouted

worked

rested

jumped

find

run

Willow's Quest

Can you use Professor Willow's time machine to turn verbs into past tense ed verbs? Write down what each past tense verb will be.

a pick   _Picked_

b climb   _climbed_

c touch   _touched_

d follow   _followed_

e kick   _Kicked_

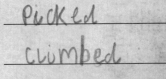

Add the owl sticker to your map, word warrior.

13

Pearl's wisdom

1 Swish, swish! Write these letters in the correct spaces in my alphabet.

a b _c_ d e _f_ g h i j k l _m_

n o _p_ q r _s_ t u v _w_ x y z

2 Use the magic within you to write down the plurals of these words.

a hand _s_____

b tree _s_____

c house _s_____

d car _s_____

e apple _s_____

f school _s_____

3 Write a sentence using each of these present tense ing verbs.

a talking _Michelangis talking to Max._

b playing _Sophia is playing with brittney_

c trying _Brittney is trying fries._

d drinking _Tilbykins drinking tea._

e singing _Tilby and brittney are singing._

f eating _sophia is eating fries with brittney_

4 Now find the word in each sentence that has the ck ending and circle it.

a Standing on the (rock,) Pearl could see the whole forest.

b Gribbit threw a (stick) for the dog to chase.

c A (flock) of birds flew over the forest.

d The fairies got a (shock) when the pixies jumped out from behind the tree.

e Gribbit went to (pick) berries.

5 These words all end with a magic e. Can you underline the vowel in the middle of each word whose sound is changed by the magic e? Just do your best!

a site   b bite   c pipe

d crate   e cane   f tone

6 Look carefully at these sentences. Put a tick in the stars beside the sentences that you think contain past tense ed verbs.

a It always rains in April. ☆

b Professor Willow rushed to post his letter. ☆

c Gem brushed Pearl's beautiful mane. ☆

d Trees drop their leaves in autumn. ☆

e Gribbit and Periwinkle asked the mice to help them to tidy their little house. ☆

Add the shells sticker to the map.

Capital letters

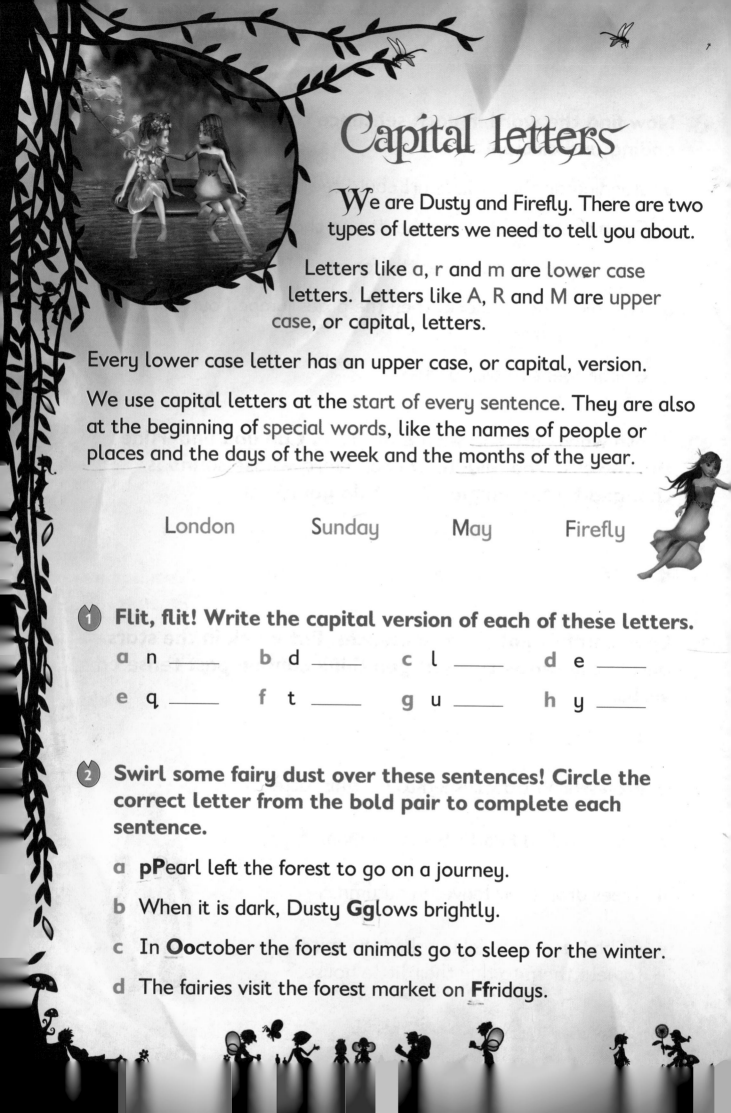

We are Dusty and Firefly. There are two types of letters we need to tell you about.

Letters like a, r and m are lower case letters. Letters like A, R and M are upper case, or capital, letters.

Every lower case letter has an upper case, or capital, version.

We use capital letters at the start of every sentence. They are also at the beginning of special words, like the names of people or places and the days of the week and the months of the year.

London   Sunday   May   Firefly

1 **Flit, flit! Write the capital version of each of these letters.**

a n _____   b d _____   c l _____   d e _____

e q _____   f t _____   g u _____   h y _____

2 **Swirl some fairy dust over these sentences! Circle the correct letter from the bold pair to complete each sentence.**

a **pP**earl left the forest to go on a journey.

b When it is dark, Dusty **Gg**lows brightly.

c In **Oo**ctober the forest animals go to sleep for the winter.

d The fairies visit the forest market on **Ff**ridays.

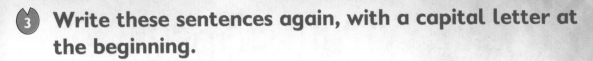

3 Write these sentences again, with a capital letter at the beginning.

a the fairies play in the garden.

The fairies play in the garden.

b four owls flew over.

Four owls flew over.

c pixies can be naughty.

Pixies can be naughty

d a full moon is very pretty.

A full moon is very beautiful.

Willow's Quest

Make a path for Gribbit by colouring in the lily pads that contain words which should begin with a capital letter.

Pop the dragonflies sticker on your map.

Full stops

My Book of Knowledge is special.

We use full stops to show our readers that a sentence has finished. Without full stops, our writing would get muddled up.

Tick-tock, full stop.

Remember that after a full stop, the next sentence must always start with a capital letter.

1 **Add a full stop to complete each of these sentences. No time like the present!**

a   The fox chased the rabbit

b   Moonlight shone on the Enchanted Forest

c   An owl swooped through the trees

d   The squirrel jumped from tree to tree

e   Two frogs croaked by the Lake of Wisdom

f   Professor Willow read a magic book

2 **Read this passage, then circle the full stops in blue and the capital letters in red.**

It was dark in the forest. An owl hooted in the distance. Baby badgers played in a clearing. A tiny mouse found an acorn to eat.

3 Wonderful work! Before you add a full stop to a sentence, you must be sure that the sentence has finished. It has to make sense. Tick the sentences that you think have finished.

a Fairies hide in the flowers.

b Pearl trotted towards.

c Gribbit and Periwinkle are friends with.

d The snails left slimy trails on the ground.

e Gem and Firefly were looking at.

f Finn wanted to visit the palace but.

g Professor Willow read the Book of Knowledge carefully.

Willow's Quest

Write your own endings for these sentences. Remember the full stop!

a At school I like _____

b My favourite colour _____

c I like to eat _____

d At the weekend I _____

e For my birthday I would like _____

Pop the hedgehogs sticker on your map.

Questions

Let's get busy! Most sentences end with a full stop, but if you are writing a question, you must end the sentence with a question mark.

Why are fairies so silly?

Using a question mark helps to let your readers know that they are reading a question.

1 **Have a look at these squelchy sentences. Put a tick in the acorn by the sentences which you think are questions.**

a When will Professor Willow be back?

b There was a full moon last night.

c Dewdrops hung in the spider's web.

d Where is Pearl going today?

e What are Gem and Firefly doing by the lake?

f Finn can talk to the animals.

g Aurora has strong wings to fly with.

2 Now have a go at adding the question mark to the end of each question. Bugalicious!

a How many snails are crawling on the ground _____

b Which animal lives in the hole in that tree _____

c Where will Pearl travel to for her next adventure _____

d Which fairy swirls pink fairy dust _____

3 Can you think of endings for these questions, smarty-pants? Don't forget the question mark!

a What time is _____

b Where is _____

c Will it _____

d When will _____

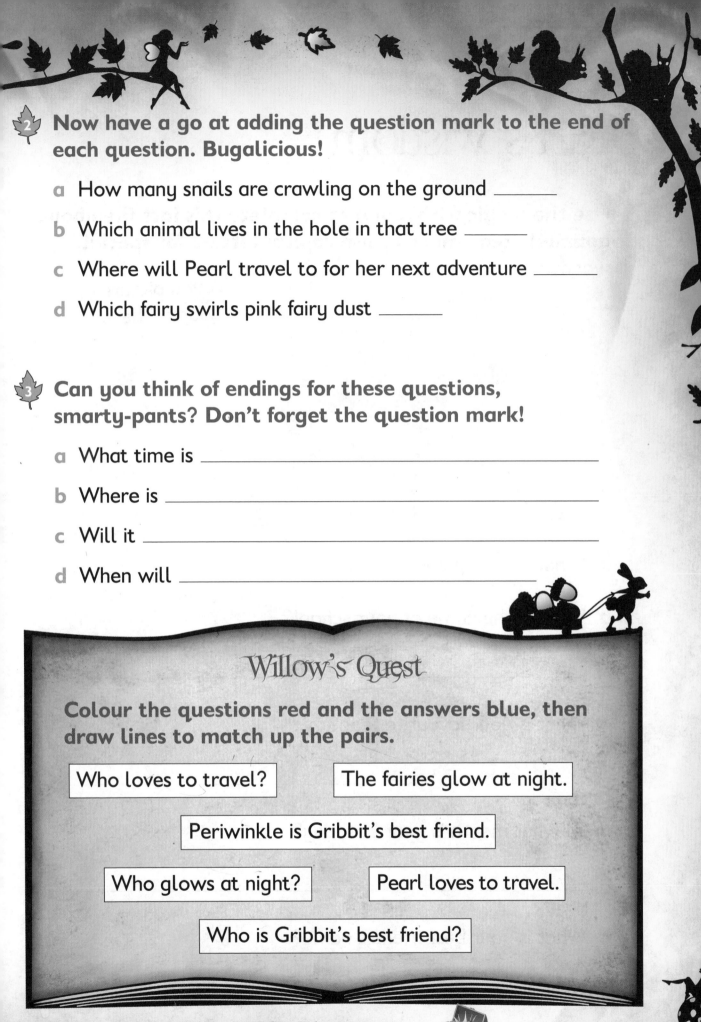

Willow's Quest

Colour the questions red and the answers blue, then draw lines to match up the pairs.

Who loves to travel?   The fairies glow at night.

Periwinkle is Gribbit's best friend.

Who glows at night?   Pearl loves to travel.

Who is Gribbit's best friend?

Pop the treasure chest sticker into the glade on your map.

Pearl's wisdom

1 **Use the magic within you to complete this fact file about yourself. Remember to use capital letters for special words.**

Draw a picture of yourself here!

a What is your name? _____

b What is the name of your school?

_____

c What is your favourite food?

_____

d In what month is your birthday?

_____

e What is your best friend's name?

_____

2 Write these sentences again, with a capital letter at the beginning and a full stop at the end.

a the Enchanted Forest is full of tiny creatures

_____

b gribbit and Periwinkle fired pine needles into the air

_____

c the Book of Knowledge is very precious

_____

d the fairies swirled fairy dust over the flowers

_____

e two squirrels played in the branches of an oak tree

_____

3 Choose either a full stop or a question mark to complete each of these sentences.

a What time does the film start _____

b The path leads to the Lake of Wisdom _____

c Pearl loves to sing beautiful songs _____

d How many ladybirds can you see _____

e Where are you going on holiday _____

f Will you go to the park tomorrow _____

Add the frog sticker! Swish, swish!

Special words

Some special words are used so often that it is important to learn how to read and write them. No time like the present! These words include the days of the week and the months of the year.

January   Thursday

Other important words are the names of colours.

green   white

Some of these words can be tricky to read and to write.

1 **Tick-tock! Read these days of the week out loud, then copy them out carefully.**

a Monday   _____

b Tuesday   _____

c Wednesday   _____

d Thursday   _____

e Friday   _____

f Saturday   _____

g Sunday   _____

2 Write the months of the year in the correct order to complete the calendar. The words are in the box to help you.

| November   April   February   December   September   July |

January

_____

March

_____

May

June

_____

August

_____

October

_____

_____

3 Wonderful work! Now see if you can label the colours of each book.

a _____

c _____

b _____

d _____

Willow's Quest

Gribbit has made five spelling mistakes in his diary. Can you circle them? It is as easy as A-B-C!

Fryday 12th Marsh
Today I saw a kingfisher by the Lake of Wisdom. It had beautiful bloo feathers and a long yelow beak to catch fish. On Sonday Periwinkle saw it catch a huge fish.

Pop the woodland picnic sticker on.

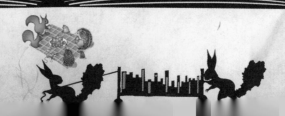

Rhyming words

Purr, purr! I am Aurora. Words with endings that sound the same rhyme.

I love to fly,
Into the sky.

Rhyming words are great for writing poems.

1 The sky is the limit with rhyming words! Draw lines to match up the pairs of words that rhyme.

a	bat	good
b	star	sail
c	wood	mat
d	tree	house
e	mouse	far
f	snail	bee

2 You are flying through this! Now see if you can write down a rhyming word for each of these.

a jam _____   d flag _____

b wall _____   e floor _____

c clown _____   f cap _____

3 Pick a word from the box to complete each of these short poems.

away	light	sings

a The forest would be dark at night,

Without the moon's pale yellow _____.

b Gem flies off on fairy wings,

While Pearl sits down and softly _____.

c The fairies always love to play,

When the pixies come they fly _____.

Willow's Quest

You are a star! Draw a picture of something that rhymes with each of these things, then write the word below it.

a cat

b hook

c goat

Find the flock of birds sticker and add it on.

Pearl's wisdom

1 **Look carefully at the words. Circle the correctly spelt word from each pair. Swish, swish!**

a Janury   January

b Orgust   August

c December   Desember

d Monday   Munday

e Thursday   Thersday

f Saterday   Saturday

g Fryday   Friday

2 Use the magic within you to add the correct colour to each sentence.

orange   black   blue   white   red   green

a Snowmen are _____.

b A carrot is _____.

c Ripe strawberries are _____.

d The sea is _____.

e Grass is _____.

f Coal is _____.

3 Complete the table below by picking words from the box which rhyme with each of the bold words in the table.

try   hop   fan   mop   buy   can   wake

sky   take   rake   man   top

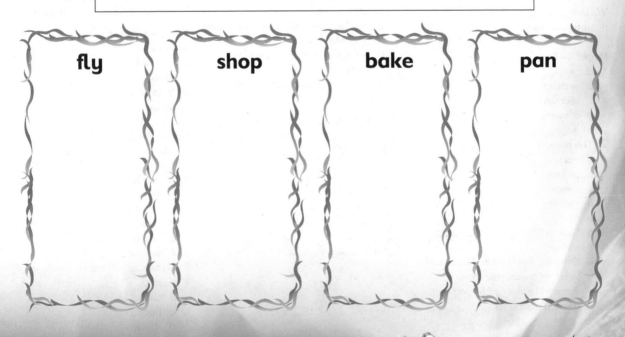

fly   **shop**   **bake**   **pan**

Finally, add your crystals sticker to complete the map!

Answers

Pages 2–3

1 The missing letters are: d, g, i, m, q, u, w and z.
2 The correct order is: a, b, f, k, p, r.
3 The correct order is: apple, ball, cat, dog.
4 The vowels are a, e, i, o and u.

Willow's Quest

The completed picture looks like this:

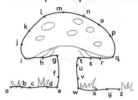

Pages 4–5

1 a bugs
  b birds
  c frogs
  d lakes
  e flowers
2 a shells
  b squirrel
  c stones
  d piles
  e conker
3 a book
  b webs
  c rabbits
  d moon
  e bats

Willow's Quest

Pictures will vary.

Pages 6–7

1 a seeing
  b wishing
  c learning
  d drawing
  e buying
2 The present tense verbs are:
  a waiting
  b picking
  c throwing
  d reading
  e flying
3 a Gem is looking into the magic mirror.
  b Drinking water from the Lake of Wisdom makes you clever.
  c Periwinkle and Gribbit say that being a pixie is fun.

d It is autumn in the Enchanted Forest and leaves are falling from the trees.
e The rabbits are sleeping in their burrows.
f Pearl is going on a long journey.

Willow's Quest

a singing
b jumping
c crying
d barking
e painting

Pages 8–9

1 a back
  b sick
  c flick
  d shock
  e lock
  f pack
2 a sock
  b brick
  c tick
  d clock
  e kick
  f sack
3 a A large black spider ran across the floor.
  b Making a wish in the Enchanted Forest brings good luck.
  c Professor Willow heard a knock at his door.
  d The fairies pick flowers in the Magic Meadow.
  e Professor Willow has a huge stack of books.
  f A flock of birds flew over the forest.
  g Gribbit showed Pearl a magic trick.

Willow's Quest

q	u	i	c	k
h	c	g	f	k
t	r	a	c	k
c	a	e	l	i
o	c	e	i	d
b	k	w	c	o
c	e	j	k	t
b	l	o	c	k

Pages 10–11

1 a stone
  b lane
  c same
  d pine
  e pile
2 a tape
  b hide
  c cape
  d ripe
  e stripe
  f rate
3 Sentences will vary.

Willow's Quest

a bone
b cone
c gate
d rope
e plate

Pages 12–13

1 a reached
  b cooked
  c waited
  d listened
  e painted
2 a The fairies <u>watched</u> the sun set.
  b Gribbit <u>laughed</u> at Periwinkle.
  c The frog <u>gobbled</u> up a fly.
  d Pearl <u>galloped</u> through the forest.
  e Professor Willow <u>turned</u> the page in the Book of Knowledge.
3 The past tense ed verbs are: washed, rested, shouted, jumped and worked.

Willow's Quest

a picked
b climbed
c touched
d followed
e kicked

Pages 14–15

1 The missing letters are: c, f, m, p, s and w.
2 a hands
  b trees
  c houses
  d cars
  e apples
  f schools
3 Sentences will vary.
4 a rock
  b stick
  c flock
  d shock

   e pick

5 a site

   b bite

   c pipe

   d crate

   e cane

   f tone

6 The sentences which contain past tense ed verbs are: b, c and e.

Pages 16–17

1 a N

   b D

   c L

   d E

   e Q

   f T

   g U

   h Y

2 a Pearl left the forest to go on a journey.

   b When it is dark, Dusty glows brightly.

   c In October the forest animals go to sleep for the winter.

   d The fairies visit the forest market on Fridays.

3 a The fairies play in the garden.

   b Four owls flew over.

   c Pixies can be naughty.

   d A full moon is very pretty.

Willow's Quest

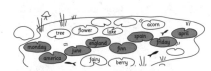

Pages 18–19

1 a The fox chased the rabbit.

   b Moonlight shone on the Enchanted Forest.

   c An owl swooped through the trees.

   d The squirrel jumped from tree to tree.

   e Two frogs croaked by the Lake of Wisdom.

   f Professor Willow read a magic book.

2 It was dark in the forest. An owl hooted in the distance. Baby badgers played in a clearing. A tiny mouse found an acorn to eat.

3 The sentences which are properly finished are: a, d and g.

Willow's Quest

Answers will vary.

Pages 20–21

1 The questions are: a, d and e.

2 a How many snails are crawling on the ground?

   b Which animal lives in the hole in that tree?

   c Where will Pearl travel to for her next adventure?

   d Which fairy swirls pink fairy dust?

3 Answers will vary.

Willow's Quest

Who loves to travel?
Pearl loves to travel.

Who is Gribbit's best friend?
Periwinkle is Gribbit's best friend.

Who glows at night?
The fairies glow at night.

Pages 22–23

1 Answers will vary, but capital letters should be used for proper nouns.

2 a The Enchanted Forest is full of tiny creatures.

   b Gribbit and Periwinkle fired pine needles into the air.

   c The Book of Knowledge is very precious.

   d The fairies swirled fairy dust over the flowers.

   e Two squirrels played in the branches of an oak tree.

3 a What time does the film start?

   b The path leads to the Lake of Wisdom.

   c Pearl loves to sing beautiful songs.

   d How many ladybirds can you see?

   e Where are you going on holiday?

   f Will you go to the park tomorrow?

Pages 24–25

1 Words should be spelt correctly.

2 The missing months, in the correct order, are: February, April, July, September, November and December.

3 a red

   b green

   c yellow

   d blue

Willow's Quest

(Fryday) 12th (Marsh)
Today I saw a kingfisher by the Lake of Wisdom. It had beautiful (bloo) feathers and a long (yelow) beak to catch fish. On (Sonday) Periwinkle saw it catch a huge fish.

Pages 26–27

1 a bat — mat
   b star — far
   c wood — good
   d tree — bee
   e mouse — house
   f snail — sail

2 Many answers are possible, including:

   a ham

   b fall

   c down

   d rag

   e door

   f map

3 a light

   b sings

   c away

Willow's Quest

Many answers are possible, including:

a hat

b book

c boat

Pages 28–29

1 a January

   b August

   c December

   d Monday

   e Thursday

   f Saturday

   g Friday

2 a white

   b orange

   c red

   d blue

   e green

   f black

3

fly	**shop**	**bake**	**pan**
try	hop	wake	fan
buy	mop	take	can
sky	top	rake	man